MIND-BOGGLERS

BIZARRE BUT AMAZINGLY TRUE TRIVIA!

Lagoon Books, London

Series Editor: Simon Melhuish
Editor: Heather Dickson
Research: Jenny Lynch, David Lever, Vicky Barber
& Simon Melhuish
Page design and layout: Linley Clode
Cover design & illustration: Gary Sherwood

Published by:
LAGOON BOOKS
PO BOX 311, KT2 5QW, UK

ISBN: 1-89971-244-5

Printed in Singapore.

MIND-BOGGLERS

BIZARRE BUT AMAZINGLY
TRUE TRIVIA!

OTHER TITLES AVAILABLE FROM LAGOON BOOKS:

GIFT BOOKS

OPTICAL ILLUSIONS & PUZZLES	(ISBN 1899712402)
AFTER DINNER GAMES	(ISBN 1899712429)
X IS FOR UNEXPLAINED	(ISBN 1899712259)

QUIZ BOOKS

WHERE IN THE WORLD AM I? - MYSTERY GEOGRAPHY QUIZ	(ISBN 1899712410)
PUB TRIVIA QUIZ	(ISBN 189971250X)
SPORTS TRIVIA QUIZ	(ISBN 1899712267)
WHO IN THE WORLD AM I? - MYSTERY CELEBRITY QUIZ	(ISBN 1899712275)

All books can be ordered from bookshops by quoting the above ISBN numbers.
Some titles may not be available in all countries. All titles are available in
the UK.

INTRODUCTION

Dozens of amazing facts, vital statistics
and naked truths from the Brazilian rain
forests to the Port of Macau, from under
the oceans to life on Mars, are revealed
in this fun-filled, fact-packed book.
To find out how long it would take Star
Trek's Enterprise to travel to the moon or
how much a rhinoceros beetle can carry
on its back, read on....

A Total of 15,000 people fainted during King George V's funeral.

Macau in China is the most densely populated place in the world with a claustrophobic **79,000** people per square mile. The UK has **611** and the USA **70** people per square mile. Greenland on the other hand has **10** square miles for every person.

In the UK, **88%** of people trust their family, **75%** trust their doctors, **22%** trust religious organisations, **15%** trust the media and **13%** trust companies but just **8%** of the population trusts the government.

On average, women utter 7,000 words per day, whereas men manage just over 2,000.

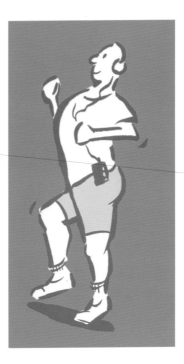

If you jog for one-and-a-half hours a day for 48 years,
you will increase your life expectancy by three years.
But unfortunately, you will have spent three years jogging!

All 15 members of a church choir were late for choir practice at a church in Beatrice, Nebraska in March 1950; they were all due to arrive at 19:20hrs, but for 10 separate, unconnected reasons, they all arrived after 19:30hrs. This was just as well for at 19:25hrs the church building was completely destroyed in an explosion.

Gordon Bennett, whose name became a common expletive, was born in 1841 and by 1876 was earning (after tax) over US$1,000,000 per year. He spent over US$40,000,000 in his lifetime on, amongst other things, the commissioning of a US$2,000,000 yacht which had a room on it specially designed for an Alderney cow to provide him milk. He once tipped a porter US$14,000. He also bought a Monte Carlo restaurant on the spot when his regular table was occupied. He immediately had the offending party evicted, sat at his table and gave the restaurant to one of the waiters. He was also the man who commissioned Stanley to find Dr Livingstone.

The Indonesian fruit bat has a wing-span equal to the height of filmstar Tom Cruise.

There are 1,600 calories in a pint of hippopotamus milk. If you chose to, you could burn these calories off by banging your head against a wall for ten-and-a-half hours.

The Eiffel Tower is **15cm** (5.9in) higher in summer than in winter. This is because the steel construction expands in the heat of the sun.

25!

It takes **25** men **14** months and **32,000** litres (7,040 gallons) of paint to cover the **20.2** hectare (50 acre) surface of the Eiffel Tower.

The total combined length of all the roots of a typical Finnish pine tree extend for 49km (30.4 miles). This is also the approximate length of the total amount of shelving in London's biggest book store, Foyles.

Ravel composed 19 hours of music in 42 years, an average of just 27 minutes per year, or four-and-a-half seconds of music per day. A complete set of Mozart's work comes to over 200 hours.

97.2% of all the Earth's water is saltwater and there is enough salt in the world's oceans to cover all the continents with a layer **150** metres (492 feet) thick.

In 1992 a phone card in Japan sold for US$42,000. It was the very first card issued in that country.

1992 1992 1992 1992 1992 1992
1992 1992 1992 1992 1992 1992
1992 1992 1992 1992 1992 1992
1992 1992 1992 1992 1992 1992
1992 1992 1992 1992 1992 1992
1992 1992 1992 1992 1992 1992
1992 1992 1992 1992 1992 1992
1992 1992 1992 1992 1992 1992
1992 1992 1992 1992 1992 1992
1992 1992 1992 1992 1992 1992
1992 1992 1992 1992 1992 1992
1992 1992 1992 1992 1992

'Warp Factor 1' on Star Trek's Enterprise, is the speed of light, or 669,600,000 miles per hour. At the other end of the scale, 'Warp factor 9' is 1516 times the speed of light, or 1,015,113,600,000 mph. At the speed of light it would take the Enterprise just 0.0645 of a second to travel from London to Sydney, or 1.2842 seconds to go to the moon.

There are about nine times as many telephone lines at the Pentagon in Washington as there are lines in Shakespeare's Hamlet. It takes less than three minutes to get through to the Pentagon and about four hours to get through Hamlet.

The human brain constitutes around **2%** of the body's weight but uses **20%** of the body's energy.

In 1938, a presidential commission concluded that the population of the United States would never reach **140** million. Twelve years later, in 1950, the population stood at **152** million.

On average, each person in the United States knows about 1,000 people. This means that if two people are picked out at random:

    i) There is a 1 in 100,000 chance that they will know each other.

    ii) There is a 1 in 100 chance that they will have an acquaintance in common.

    iii) The chance that one of them will have an acquaintance who knows someone else who knows the other person is a staggering 99 in 100 (a virtual certainty)!

The New York Herald Tribune, 14 March 1962, reported that a Mr Warren Rogers was washing the outside of a window on the third floor of the Fox Medical Building when the safety hook came undone. He was left hanging by one strap 12.2 metres (40 feet) above the ground. He was able to pull himself to safety and decided that the odds of a repeat occurrence were very low so he

resumed work. He got as far as the fifth floor when the safety hook broke again. This time he was hanging 19.8 metres (65 feet) above ground level. He decided not to make a third attempt.

In a survey **1,000** London taxi drivers were asked what their response would be if they were told that life had been found on Mars. **72%** said they didn't care.

The World Bank estimates that the annual per capita income in Vietnam in **1990** averaged just **US$ 230.**

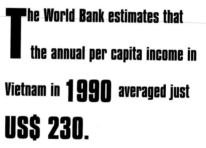

If there are 23 people gathered in one room, the probability that at least two people share the same birthday (day and month) is slightly better than 1 in 2. If there are 40 people then the probability rises to a 9 in 10 chance – very likely. With 100 people it's a virtual certainty that at least two people share a birthday.

Roy C Sullivan of Virginia, USA, was struck by lightning seven times during his life. He suffered a burnt left shoulder, legs, chest and stomach, set fire to his hair twice and lost a toenail and both eyebrows.

Psychologist Stanley Milgram conducted an experiment with a group of people in the USA in which each person was given a parcel which they had to get to a "target" person, who was someone unknown to them who lived in a distant state. They were to mail the parcel to a "friend" (someone they knew on a first name basis) who in turn either sent it to the target, if they knew them, or sent it to another friend and so on until it got to the target person. The number of intermediate links needed before the parcel reached the target averaged a surprisingly low five.

10 May 1975 was Washington D.C.'s Human Kindness Day. Police report that there were **600** arrests, **150** broken windows, **42** lootings, **120** cases of public brawling, **33** fires and **17** stonings of uniformed officers that day.

Murder was the grisly cause of most deaths in car-repair shops, car showrooms and filling stations in the United States in 1995. It was the second biggest cause of death amongst teenage girls in Massachusetts; the first was accidents involving cars.

Brendan Maguire was voted sheriff of San Mateo County, California in 1986 with an overwhelming majority of 81,679. Unfortunately he had been dead for two months.

$7,360

According to Professor Fox of the University of Wisconsin, USA, playing slot machines really is a mug's game: on a typical machine with three dials and twenty symbols, you can expect to win back a rather disappointing US$7,360 for every US$10,000 you 'invest'.

Polar bears can run at speeds of 40km per hour (24.8mph) for short stretches, jump lengths of at least 3.7 metres (12.1 feet) and heights of up to 2 metres (6.6 feet). Their high jump is only slightly off Olympic standards.

A lettuce leaf is **94%** water, a human being **60–70%** water and a pine tree **55%**. Approximately **2,800** litres (616 gallons) of water goes into growing **1kg** of rice (2.2lbs).

An amazing coincidence happened in June 1944, just before the Allied invasion of Europe during World War II. The army was planning a top secret campaign littered with codewords. The campaign was known as OVERLOAD and its naval spearhead went by the name NEPTUNE. The troops were to land at points known as UTAH and OMAHA and the harbours used to supply the troops were

disguised by the name MULBERRY. Astonishingly enough, in the 33 days leading up to D-Day each of these words appeared as answers in the crossword in The Daily Telegraph, a UK national paper, with the key word "overload" appearing just four days before the troops landed. Crossword compiler Leonard Dawe had a hard time trying to convince nervous security officials that he was completely unaware of the significance of the words.

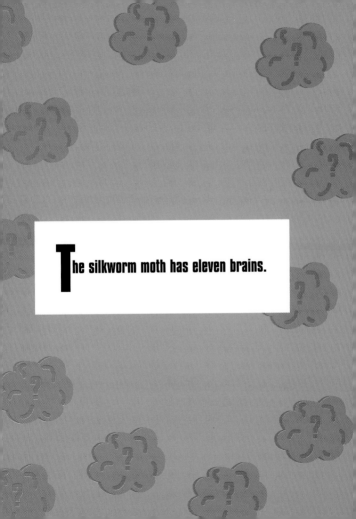

The silkworm moth has eleven brains.

The Titanic weighed **46,329** tons. It very nearly collided with the moored liner "The New York" and another ship, "The Teutonic", in the first few minutes after it left Southampton on its disastrous maiden voyage in 1912.

There are at least 250,000,000 bubbles waiting to burst out of every bottle of champagne.

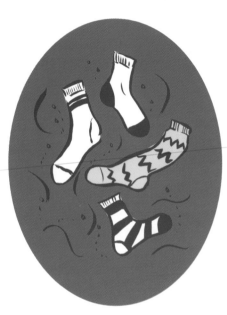

There are just over 100,000,000 adult men in the USA. If each man loses two socks per year in the wash, the number of odd socks kicking around the United States increases by a staggering 400,000,000 socks per year. Where do they all go?

1898

In 1898 Morgan Robertson published a novel about a ship called "The Titan", the story of a liner which sank on its maiden voyage when it hit an iceberg. This was fourteen years before the sinking of the Titanic. Amazingly, both fictional and real ships were of the same tonnage and disappeared in the same ocean. Neither had sufficient lifeboats.

A 1976 survey, "Gambling In America", showed that families with incomes of under US$10,000 spent ten times as much on lotteries (expressed as a percentage of their income) than families earning over US$30,000.

In 1976, Jacquy Nuguet plunged 10 people in Nice, France, into a hypnotically-induced sleep. They stayed asleep for 10 days.

300 women in the UK have insured themselves against the possibility of a Virgin Birth which they fear might happen at the turn of the century.

In 1899 Canadian actor Charles Coghlan died in Galveston in the USA some 5,600km (3,480 miles) away from his home in Prince Edward Island. He was buried in a lead coffin which was placed in a granite vault. In September 1900, a hurricane hit Galveston flooding the vault and the coffin floated out of the Gulf of Mexico and into the Atlantic Ocean. The Gulf stream carried it along for eight years until October 1908, when it was spotted by a local fisherman on Prince Edward Island. His body had returned home nine years after his death.

Over **9,000,000** people die each year in India, while only **7,800,000** die in China, yet China's population is **32%** larger than India's.

Beetles are the strongest animals in proportion to their size - a rhinoceros beetle can carry 850 times its own weight on its back.

If you take out a £100,000 mortgage on a 25 year term, at an average interest rate of 10% per year, you will have paid a hefty £272,610.22 to repay the loan by the end of the 25 years.

Engineers at ICI reportedly spent some time in the 1970s investigating the theory that a dropped piece of buttered toast was most likely to land butter-side down. To their astonishment, they discovered what they labelled 'the perversity factor': the results were completely random if the toast landed on a washable surface; if it landed on a carpet, however, it was more likely to land butter-side down.

Average life expectancy in industrialised countries is now 74.6 years. Life expectancy in developing countries is 62.4 years, as opposed to an average of just 44.2 years in 1960.

More people have heart attacks and more cars break down on a Monday than any other day of the week.

In 1986, 4,000,000 Americans were alcoholics.

In 1963, the former James Bond star Sean Connery backed number **17** three times running at the roulette table in Italy's St Vincent casino. He won in true 007 style, despite odds against him winning of **50,652** to **1**.

Composer John Cage wrote a piano composition entitled 4 minutes 33 seconds. It is made up of four minutes and 33 seconds of total silence during which time the composer sits completely still. Mr Cage explained that his composition lasts for 273 seconds and -273C is absolute zero, the temperature at which all molecules stop moving.

Over 67% of people admit to urinating while in public swimming pools.

It's good to talk, at least in Monaco, where each person has an average of 1.7 telephones. The queue for the phone in Zaire could be a long one though for there's only one phone per 1,000 people.

Don't leave your car unlocked in the UK as it has the highest car theft rate in the world (almost **1%** of all cars are stolen each year).

In Nepal you might as well leave the keys in the ignition as there's a **1** in **5,000,000** chance of it being stolen.

1992

The number of deaths in India peaked in **1992**, when an average of **24,663** deaths were recorded each day.

If a couple have four children, the most likely combination of boys and girls is not, as you might think, two of each sex. There are 16 possible combinations, six of which are two of each sex, which represents a 3 in 8 chance of two boys and two girls. The possibility of three of one sex occurs eight times, and four of all the same sex occurs twice, so there is a 5 in 8 chance that the couple will have something other than two boys & two girls - much more likely.

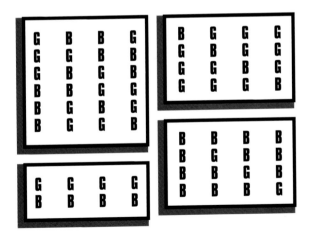

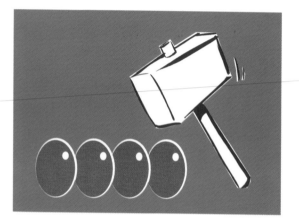

Warninks, makers of the egg-based liquor Advocaat, has an egg breaking department that separates the yolks from the whites at a rate of 18,000 eggs per hour.

If you commute to work every day, taking an hour to get there and an hour to get home – between the ages of **22** and **65** – you will have spent a staggering two-and-a-half years in transit. These figures do not even allow for delays, strikes or traffic jams.

In 1974 Bramber Parish Council in England decided to go without street lighting for three days to save money. Afterwards, the treasurer was pleased to announce that, as a result, electricity to the value of £11.59 had been saved. He added, however, that there was an £18.48 bill for switching the electricity off and another of £12.00 for switching it on again. It had cost the council £18.89 to spend three days in darkness.

Not only does the USA have the most television channels, it has the most TVs as well – 813 per 1,000 people, or 201,000,000 sets in total. In Mali there is just 1 set per 2,500 people.

China is the world's

biggest manufacturer of TVs,

turning out almost 28,000,000

sets a year.

A survey of the way in which the French press presented the British Royal Family, between 1958 and 1972, came up with the following statistics. The Queen was pregnant 92 times, had 149 accidents, 19 miscarriages and took the pill 11 times. She abdicated 63 times and was on the point of breaking up with Prince Philip 73 times. She was said to be fed up 112 times and on the verge of a nervous breakdown 32 times. She had 43 unhappy nights, 27 nightmares and her life was threatened 29 times. She was rude to the Queen of Persia 11 times and to Princess Grace of Monaco 6 times.

In one UK supermarket, **13** women became pregnant after manning till number **11**. The management renamed the till **10a**.

In 1995, traces of cocaine were found on 40% of all used banknotes returned to the Bank of England. In the USA the figure was almost 75%.

In Malaysia, more people are killed by falling coconuts than from poisonous snake bites.

92% of drivers who cause death or bodily harm, drive after using alcohol or drugs, drive dangerously or break the speed limit, are male.

People in Singapore buy more shoes than the inhabitants of any other country (6.82 pairs per person per year), but spend only US$5.1 per pair compared to the Germans who spend US$42.6 per pair on their 4.5 pairs of shoes. Indians buy the least – 0.41 pairs – and spend only 91 cents per pair.

In 1991, Americans spent US$31,000,000,000 (£20,666,000,000) on shoes.

A cat has 32 muscles in each ear.

Finland has the highest rate of fraud in the world, with **2,064** frauds reported per **100,000** people.

15% of the world's fresh water flows down the Amazon river, but only **0.4%** of the world's population have access to it.

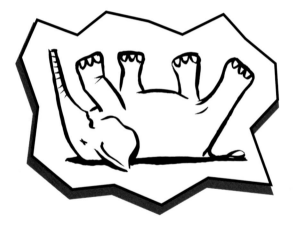

The first bomb the Allies dropped on Berlin during World War II killed the only elephant in the city's zoo.

The American UFO Insurance Company issues certificates of insurance against abduction by aliens. For the very reasonable sum of US$20 you are insured for US$10,000,000 in the event of being seized. All you need to claim the cash is the signature of the alien abductor.

London insurance firm GRIP also insures against alien abduction but for the higher premium of **£102** (US$153). Its policy, however, also covers you against alien impregnation or turning into a vampire or even a werewolf.

The homicide capital of the world is Swaziland with one murder per **1,139** people, per year. The USA is relatively safe with one murder per **10,638** people. Argentina, perhaps surprisingly, is the world's safest place with just one murder for every **714,285** people.

The sperm count of the average Finnish male is double the world average. The average number of children per Finnish couple, however, is just 1.8.

The sweet-toothed British eat 624,000,000 Mars bars and 170,000,000 packets of fruit pastilles a year.

According to the British Medical Journal, the risk of death from smoking cigarettes is equivalent to being pricked with an HIV infected needle three times every year. This theory is based on the fact that there is a 45% risk of death from HIV needle injury over 42 years, a time span in which tobacco is said to kill half its regular users.

1996

The verification of alien life on 8 August 1996, when the discovery of fossilised microscopic life in a Martian meteorite was announced, meant that Steve Upton from North London won **£1,000** from a **£10** bet made on 22 August 1995, that alien life would be verified within a year.

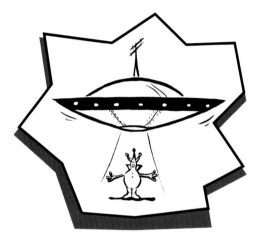

The average number of witnesses to a UFO sighting is 2.2; of these 68% are male.

Koalas are the laziest animals in the world – they sleep for 22 hours a day.

The drops of water in fog are so small that it would take 7,000,000,000 to create a teaspoonful of water.

Ireland has the highest per capita calorie consumption in the world at **3,952** calories per person per day. No-one seems sure how much of that comes from the Guinness!

An alarming 1,750,000 men, women and children are reported missing each year in Europe. Of these only 35% are ever accounted for.

In Rio de Janeiro, in Brazil, there are more plastic surgeons than there are public health doctors.

The chance of a Bridge player being dealt a complete suit of **13** cards is a mere **1** in **158,753,389,900**.

1994

If every member of every 1994 West End play audience had sent a postcard to a different person in Belgium, every Belgian would have received a postcard.

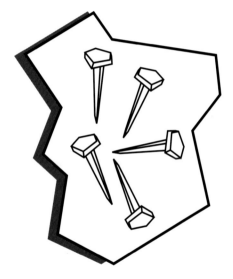

If all the wasted nails in discarded wooden pallets around the world were recycled, they could make 380,000 car bodies.

SOURCES

The Guinness Book of Records

How to Lie With Statistics, *Darel Huff*

Lady Luck: Theory of Probability, *Warren Weaver*

Aha Gotcha!, *Martin Gardner*

Not a lot of People Know That, Either, *Michael Caine*

Magic Tricks and Mathematics, *Martin Gardner*

Bizarre Books, *Russell Ash & Brian Lake*

The Encyclopaedia of Gambling, *Peter Arnold*

Gambling, A Guardian Guide, *Julian Arnold*

Great Disasters, *John Canning*

Unexplained Mysteries

Lies, Damned Lies and Some Exclusives, *Henry Porter*

The Book of Heroic Failures and
The Return of Heroic Failures, *Stephen Pile*

All the Trouble in the World, *P J O'Rourke*

The Alien World, *Peter Brookesmith*

The SAS Survival handbook, *John Wiseman*

The Top 10 of Everything, *Russell Ash*

Times Book of Answers, *Christopher Lloyd*

Also: New Statesman, Scientific American, Times, The Daily Mail, Which?, Readers Digest, The Daily Telegraph, The Times, The Guardian, The Big Issue, Computer Life, Cosmopolitan, Encyclopaedia Americana, FHM, Marie Claire, Maxim, & New Scientist.